COST OF CAPITAL

I0503341

COST OF FUNDS

Toye Adelaja

COST OF CAPITAL

Copyright © 2015 by (Toye Adelaja)

All rights reserved. No part of this book may be reproduced or transmitted in any form or by any means without written permission from the author.

ISBN (978 1516849055)

INTRODUCTION

Cost of capital is very important to both the users of funds and the providers of funds. It is used by investors to determine the viability and profitability of their investments.

Many investors and borrowers of funds do not know much about a cost of capital. This is the reason this book has been written to demystify and explain clearly the cost of capital.

TABLE OF CONTENTS

CHAPTER 1

Introduction to Cost of Capital

Capital can also be called fund or finance. A business owner has to finance his or her business. How and where can he get the capital or fund to execute his business? How and where to get the capital or funds is referred to as sources of capital or sources of finance.

If a business is financed solely by the funds contributed by the owners of the business, this source of finance is called equity finance. If the business is financed by the funds borrowed from external institutions or individuals, it is called debt finance. Where a business is financed by both equity and debt, we call it debt equity finance.

The owner of the fund has other alternative avenue in which his fund can be invested. If a fund is invested in a particular business, the return or gain such fund should have realized if it has been invested in other venture is called the cost of the fund. We can also say that a cost of capital is the return lost for not investing in an alternative business. Cost of capital can therefore be defined as an alternative return forgone.

The concept of cost of capital is a return or yield concept. It means that the return from each fund is used as the numerator while the current market value of the fund for the period under consideration is used as the denominator. It can be represented in most cases as

Yield or Return =   Income

                    Investment

Various sources of finance with their respective income, are demonstrated below:

Souces of Funds	Income
Equity	Dividend
Retained Earnings	Dividend
Preference Shares	Fixed dividend
Debentures	Fixed interest
Short Term loans	Interest
Bank Overdraft	Interest

CHAPTER 2

COST OF EQUITY

Cost of Equity refers to the returns due to ordinary shareholders or common stockholders for making funds available for the operation of a company over a given financial period. It can also be referred to what the company has to give up in order to make use of ordinary shareholders' funds or common stockholder's funds.

2. Cost of Equity can be determined in the following circumstances:

1. When there is a constant dividend rate.

2. When an issue cost, transaction cost, floatation cost or cost of reduction in market value per share is involved.

3. When there is growth in the rate of dividend.

2.1.1. Determination of Cost of Equity when there is a constant

dividend.

This model assumes payment of a constant annual dividend per share into an indefinite future time. This model can be called dividend valuation model.

$$Ke = \frac{d}{MVex\text{-}div} \times 100\%$$

Where:

Ke   = Cost of Equity

d   = Dividend

MVex-div   = Market value excluding dividend

NOTE:

Students always get confused with the specific market value to be used as the denominator. There are two types of market values. One is MVex-div while the other one is MVcum-div. MVex –div means market value excluding dividend while MVcum-div means market value including dividend.

The Market value that is used as a denominator is always excluding dividend. It is represented as MVex-div.

Ex- dividend is a classification of trading shares in which the seller of the shares, and not the buyer has received the dividend declared. When a market value of a share is classified as ex-dividend, it means that the dividend has actually been paid.

Cum-dividend is a type of dividend in which the buyer of a security is entitled to receive dividend which has been declared but not yet paid. Cum-div means " with dividend". A stock trades cum-dividend until the ex-dividend date.

ILLUSTRATION 1

Godam Plc has 400,000   £0.5 ordinary shares currently valued at £0.8 cumulative dividend, and the dividend which is about to be paid is £0.08. What is the company's cost of equity?

SUGGESTED SOLUTION

$$Ke = \frac{d}{MV\ ex\text{-}div} \times 100\%$$

$$= \frac{£0.08}{£0.8 - 0.08} \times 100\%$$

$$= \frac{0.08}{0.72} \times 100\%$$

$$= \quad 11.11\%$$

The Cost of Equity capital is 11.11%

NOTE!

The market value of the equity given in the above question is including a dividend because the question states that the dividend is about to be paid. It means that the dividend has not been paid. As a result of this, dividend should be deducted from the market value so that the market value would be excluding dividend.

Where a question states that dividend has already been paid, it means that the market value is excluding dividend. As a result of this, there is no need to deduct the dividend again from the market value.

Where the market value of equity given in the question is MVex-div, it means the market value is excluding dividend. You do not need to deduct dividend again because it has already been deducted from the market value of the equity.

MVex-div is the market value excluding dividend. If the market value includes the next dividend to be paid, the market value will be MVcum-div.

ILLUSTRATION 2

PY Plc. has 250,000 shares with market value of £500,000. Dividend previously paid was £0.6. Calculate the cost of equity.

SUGGESTED SOLUTION

$$Ke = \quad \frac{d}{MVex\text{-}div} \quad \times 100\%$$

$$= \quad \frac{£0.6}{} \quad \times \ 100\%$$

£2

= 30%

The Cost of Equity is 30%.

Workings:

Market value per share = £500,000

250,000

= £2

NOTE:

The market value given is excluding dividend because dividend has already been paid out previously.

2.1.2. When issue cost or transaction cost is involved

When there is issue cost, transaction cost or cost of floatation of shares, the formula for the calculation of cost of equity will be modified as follows:

$$Ke = \frac{d}{(MVex\text{-}div) - c}$$

Where:

c= issue cost or cost of transaction

ILLUSTRATION 3

ZP International Ltd. has 300,000 shares of £0.90 per share. The market value per share is £6 cum-div. Dividend declared is £0.95 per share. ZP issued additional shares of 60,000 and incurred issuing cost of £0.10 per share.

Calculate the Cost of Equity

SUGGESTED SOLUTION

$$Ke = \frac{d}{(MVex\text{-}div) - c} \times 100\%$$

$$= \frac{£0.95}{(£6 - £0.95) - £0.10} \times 100\%$$

$$= \frac{0.95}{4.95} \times 100\%$$

$$= 19.19\%$$

2.1.3. When there is a growth in dividend rate

Shareholders always expect their dividend to increase over time instead of remaining constant indefinitely. Where there is a growth in dividend, it means that the dividend is no longer constant. Therefore, an element of a growth in dividend has to be included in the formula for calculating cost of equity. The formula is called Gordon's Growth Model.

$$Ke = \frac{d_0(1 + g)}{MVex\text{-}div} + g \times 100\%$$

Where:

Ke   =   Cost of Equity

d_0 =   current dividend

g   =   growth rate

MVex-div =   Market value excluding dividend

NOTE!

Where the dividend has just been paid or is a current dividend, this is d_0 and must be adjusted for growth rate during year 1 to become $d_0(1 + g)^1$.

The formula can also be written as follows:

$$Ke = \frac{d_1}{MVex\text{-}div} + g \times 100\%$$

NOTE!

The formula above is adopted where dividend for the next year is known. The dividend for the next year is represented by d_1.

Where:

Ke = Cost of Equity

d_1 = dividend to be paid for next year.

ILLUSTRATION 4

Webcity International Corporation has in issue 24 million ordinary shares with a market value of £14 per share. £12 million were paid as dividend this year which represented 75% of earnings. The earnings are expected to grow at an annual rate of 10%. The issue of new ordinary shares now will make the company to incur cost which would represent £0.50 per share and a reduction below market value of £1 per share would also be made.

Calculate the company's cost of equity?

SUGGESTED SOLUTION

The first thing we need to do is to calculate dividend paid per share:

Dividend per share = $\dfrac{\text{Total dividend paid}}{\text{Number of ordinary share}}$

= $\dfrac{£12,000,000}{24,000,000}$

= £0.5

Calculation of cost of equity:

$$Ke = \left(\frac{do(1+g)}{MVex\text{-}div - c - r} + g \right) \times 100\%$$

$$= \frac{(0.5(1+0.1)}{14 - 0.5 - 1} + 0.1) \times 100\%$$

$$= \frac{(0.5(1.1)}{14 - 1.5} + 0.1) \times 100\%$$

$$= \frac{(0.55)}{12.5} + 0.1) \times 100\%$$

$$= (0.044 + 0.1) \times 100\%$$

$$= 0.144 \times 100\%$$

$$= 14.4\%$$

2.1.4 Calculation of Growth Rate
ILLUSTRATION 5

Bravo Ltd. paid dividends in the past five years as follows:

	£
2004	120,000
2003	118,000
2002	108,000
2001	104,000
2000	100,000

You are required to calculate the growth rate in dividend.

SUGGESTED SOLUTION

Growth rate:

Year 2000 div.$(1+g)^4$ = Year 2004 div.

$£100,000(1+g)^4$ $= £120,000$

$$\frac{£100,000(1+g)^4}{£100,000} = \frac{£120,000}{£100,000}$$

$(1+g)^4$ $= 1.2$

$1+g$ $= \sqrt[4]{1.2}$

$1+g$ $= 1.0466$

g $= 1.0466 - 1$

g $= 0.0466$

g $= 4.66\%$

The growth rate is 4.66%.

NOTE:

The year 2000 is assumed to be year 0, year 2001 is assumed to be year 1, year 2002 is assumed to be year 2, year 2003 is assumed to be year 3, year 2004 is assumed to be year 4.

Estimation of Growth Rate from Retained Earnings (Gordon's growth rate model)

$$g = R \times b$$

Where:

g = Growth rate in dividends

R = Return from retained earnings

b = Percentage of earnings retained

ILLUSTRATION 6

PZ Plc. has a policy of retaining 40% of earnings annually. If the expected returns from earnings is 15% per annum. What is the growth in dividend?

SUGGESTED SOLUTION

g   = Rb

$$= 40\% \times 15\%$$

$$= 0.06 \times 100$$

$$= 6\%$$

2.2. Calculation of Cost of Equity using Capital Assets Pricing Model (CAPM)

The CAPM is an alternative approach to the problem of computing cost of capital, more especially cost of equity. The motive is to determine linear relationship between risk and return in the capital market.

The CAPM could be used to calculate cost of equity.

The formula is stated below:

$$Rr = Rt + ß(Rm - Rt)$$

Where:

Rr is the required rate of return of a security

Rt is the risk-free rate of return

Rm is the expected return of the market portfolio

ß is the beta co-efficient of the security

Note:

The risk-free rate is the rate desired from a security which is totally free of risk.

The ß co-efficient is found by dividing the covariance of the return on the new investment and the return on the market portfolio by the variance of the market return.

$$ß = \frac{Cov\ (Rt.\ Rm)}{Variance\ (Rm)}$$

More of the CAPM would be discussed under investment portfolio management.

ILLUSTRATION 1

If the risk free interest rate is 8%, the market return is 12% and the beta co-efficient is 1.2. Calculate the cost of equity.

SOLUTION:

$Rr = Rt + ß (Rm - Rt)$

$Rr = 0.08 + 1.2(0.12 - 0.08)$

$\quad = 0.128$

$\quad = 12.8\%$

The cost of capital estimated according to capital asset pricing model is 12.8%.

CHAPTER 3

COST OF RETAINED EARNINGS

Retained earnings are the accumulated reserves and other revenues retained in business, which legitimately belong to ordinary shareholders or common stockholders. Retained earnings which form a component of a **capital structure** of a business entity, is the part of earnings available to ordinary shareholders, not paid out as dividend. Retained earnings can also be called the accumulation of profit retained in business, or profit plowed back into the business for the expansion of business.

There is a cost to the common stockholders who do not collect the whole profit made by the business as dividend, but decide to retain some part of it in the business for the expansion. This cost is called a cost of retained earnings.

What is the cost of retained earnings? The cost of retained earnings is equal to the cost of equity. Cost of retained earnings is equal to the **cost of equity** because ordinary shareholders are both the provider of equity fund and retained earnings, and hence the cost of the two funds should be the same for the providers.

How do we calculate the cost of retained earnings? The formula for the calculation of cost of retained earnings is explained below:

$$Ke = \frac{d}{MVex\text{-}div} \times 100\%$$

Complexity of Cost of Retained Earnings

The complexity of cost of retained earnings will be seen in the calculation of **Weighted Average Cost of Capital**. Where cost of each fund is attached to the market value of each fund in calculating weighted average cost of capital, retained earnings will be excluded from the calculation. The reason is that the shareholders would have adjusted for the retained earnings in arriving at the market value of company's ordinary shares.

CHAPTER 4

COST OF PREFERENCE SHARES

Preference shareholders are not part of the owners of a company. They are merely shareholders therefore; there is a need to pay them fixed dividends as returns on their investments. Preference shareholders are commonly referred to as Preferred stockholders in the USA. The owners of preference shares have prior right to a company's dividends and refund of capital in case of liquidation of company, over the ordinary shareholders or common stockholders.

Taxation is not applicable in the calculation of cost of preference shares. The reason is that the dividends on **preference shares** are charged to the profit after tax.

Face value or par value of a preference share is the value or price per preference share stated on the share certificate. Dividend per preference share can be calculated by multiplying the rate of a dividend payable on preference share by the face value or par value of the preference share. Market value of preference shares might not be the same as the face value of the preference shares depending on the financial situation of the company. The values of dividends payable on preference shares are computed as follows:

Dividends payable =Dividend rate × Face value × No. of preference shares

Dividend payable per share   = dividend rate × face value of a preference share

Preference shares can be classified into irredeemable and redeemable preference shares. Irredeemable preference shares are perpetual and have no maturity date while redeemable preference shares are the preference shares that have maturity date.

4.1. Cost of Irredeemable Preference Shares

$$Kp = \frac{d}{MVex\text{-}div} \times 100\%$$

Where :

Kp = Cost of preference share

d = fixed dividend

MV ex-div = market value of preference share excluding dividend

ILLUSTRATION 1

Jasco Plc. has 400,000 6% preference shares of £1 per share which were originally issued at £0.92 per share. The current price is 43%. However, if similar issue is made now, it would be valued at £0.40 per share. Compute the cost of preference shares.

SUGGESTED SOLUTION

$$Kp = \frac{d}{MVex\text{-}div} \times 100\%$$

$$= \frac{£\ 0.06}{£0.4} \times 100\%$$

$$= 0.15 \times 100\%$$

$$= 15\%$$

Workings:

1) Determination of dividend

d = dividend rate × face value of preference share

$$= 6\% \times £1$$

$$= £0.06$$

NOTE:

The above preference share is irredeemable preference share because it has no maturity date.

4.2. Cost of Redeemable Preference Share

Cost of Redeemable Preference Share is that rate of return that equates the current market value of preference share with the sum of discounted value of all future preference dividends and the discounted value of market value of preference share at redemption date. This can be calculated in the same way as the cost of convertible debenture and redeemable debenture. The following are relevant in the calculation of cost of redeemable preference shares:

The most current total market value of the preference shares at the time of issue

The flow of dividends from the time of issue of the share to the maturity date

The market value of preference share at redemption or maturity date

CHAPTER 5

COST OF DEBENTURE

A debenture is a component of a capital structure of a firm. A debenture certificate is issued by companies to raise long term loans which cannot be provided by the owners of the companies to finance capital project. It can also be referred to as secured loan stocks. The provider of the long term loan is called a debenture holder. A debenture holder is entitled to periodic fixed returns on the investment of his or her funds. The fixed return is called interest.

Characteristics of a debenture are as follows:

1. Debenture is a long term fund.

2. The face value or par value of debenture is the price at which one unit of debenture is issued.

3. Par value of a debenture is normally in £100 in the UK and $1,000 in the US.

4. Interest rate is known with certainty.

5. Interest per unit of debenture is known (interest rate × par value of debenture).

6. Total interest on debenture is known (interest rate × par value × Units of debentures).

7. Adjustment should be made for tax in the interest element and not in the market value.

8. The most recent market value is known.

Debentures can be classified into irredeemable, redeemable and convertible debentures. Each type of debenture has a specific cost of capital. There are many other types of debentures.

5.1. Cost of Irredeemable Debentures

The formula of cost of irredeemable debenture is described below:

$$Kd = \frac{i}{MVex\text{-}int - c} \times 100\%$$

Where the element of taxation is to be incorporated, the cost of irredeemable debenture will now be:

$$Kd = \frac{i(1-t)}{MVex\text{-}int - c} \times 100\%$$

Where:

i = interest

MVex-int = Current market value of debenture excluding interest

c = Cost of issuing debenture

t = tax rate

ILLUSTRATION 1

JV Plc has issued 4.5% 3,000,000 debenture stock at par in 1998. The current market price is £46. If a similar issued is to be made now, it would be made at £45. Tax rate is given as 25%. Determine the cost of debenture.

SUGGESTED SOLUTION

$$Kd = \frac{i(1-t)}{MVex\text{-}int} \times 100\%$$

$$= \frac{4.5(1-0.25)}{45} \times 100\%$$

$$= \frac{4.5(0.75)}{45} \times 100\%$$

$$= \frac{3.375}{45} \times 100\%$$

$$= 0.075 \times 100\%$$

$$= 7.5\%$$

The cost of irredeemable debenture is 7.5%

NOTE :

Most current market value should be used as the denominator.

Par value of debenture is always in £100 in the UK.

Workings

Calculation of interest par unit of debenture:

i = Interest rate × par value of debenture

$$= 4.5\% \times £100$$

$$= £4.5$$

5.2. Cost of Redeemable Debenture

The cost of redeemable debenture is the discount factor or cost of capital that equates the current market value with the addition of expected future interests and the market value at the date of redemption of debenture. It means that we have to calculate **Internal Rate of Return (IRR)**. IRR is the discount factor that will make Net Present value (NPV) to be Zero.

Procedures for calculating IRR:

a. Identify the most current market value of the debenture. This is the market value for year Zero

b. Identify all the expected interests.

c. Identify its market value at the date of redemption.

d. Identify the number of years at the end of which it will be redeemed.

e. Choose a discount rate that will give a negative **Net present Value (NPV)**

f. Choose another discount rate that will give a positive **Net present Value (NPV)**

$$IRR = LR + \frac{(NPVH)}{NPVH+NPVL} \times (HR - LR) \times 100\%$$

Where :

IRR   = Internal Rate of Return

LR   = Lower discount rate (-)

HR   = Higher discount rate (+)

NPVH   = Higher NPV

NPVL   = Lower NPV

CHAPTER 6

WEIGHTED AVERAGE COST OF CAPITAL (WACC)

What is the ideal cost of capital to be used by a company that obtains funds from different sources to finance a project? The project can be an acquisition of new machinery, building of a factory etc. The cost of capital for each source of finance taken in isolation is irrelevant. However, the ideal cost of capital, is the cost of capital that combines all other cost of capital such as cost of equity, retained earnings, preference shares, debentures and other long term loan. This ideal cost of capital is called weighted average cost of capital. The weighted average cost of capital is the weighted average of the cost of various components of the company's **capital structure**. The weights attached are based on the proportion that each component contributes to the total capital structure of the company.

Where a company is financed by only one source of finance, the WACC will be the cost of the fund only. For example, where a company is financed by equity alone, the WACC will be the cost of the equity.

How do you calculate WACC?

The general formula for the calculation of WACC is demonstrated below:

a) $WACC = \dfrac{\text{Total Return}}{\text{Total Market Value}}$

The formula above can be further expanded below.

$$WACC = \frac{Ve \times Ke}{V} + \frac{Vp \times Kp}{V} + \frac{Vd \times Kd(1 - T)}{V}$$

Where:
Ve = current market value of equity
Ke = cost of equity
V   = total market value; the addition of the market values of all long term funds

Vd = current market value of debenture
Kd = cost of debenture
Vp = current market value of preference share
Kp = cost of preference share
T = corporation tax

NOTE:

The formula above can only be used where element of tax has not been considered in the determination of cost of debenture. Where element of tax has been considered in the determination of cost of debenture, the formula will be excluded of $(1 - T)$. The formula will be:

$$WACC = \frac{Ve \times Ke}{V} + \frac{Vp \times Kp}{V} + \frac{Vd \times Kd}{V}$$

NOTE:

Only capital should be used in the calculation of WACC. Short term loan or short term fund will not be included in the calculation of WACC. The reasons are as follows:

i.   Short term loans are not traded on the capital market and hence, they have no market value.

ii. Cost of short term funds are not included in the evaluation of capital project.

Retained earnings and reserves should also be excluded in the calculation of WACC because cost of equity has already taken care of retained earnings. Cost of equity or common stock is equal to cost of retained earnings.

Total market value of equity can also be referred to as market capitalization.

ILLUSTRATION 1

Vicky Plc. has a capital structure consisting of 200,000 £1 ordinary shares, and 100,000 12% loan stock. The ordinary shares are currently valued at £0.75 each and the loan stock at £80. Annual dividends have been constantly running at £0.10 per share and a dividend has just been paid too.

a) Calculate:
   i.   Cost of equity
   ii.   Cost of loan stock
   iii. Weighted average cost of capital

b) Advise the management of Vicky Plc. on the relevant and ideal cost of capital to use in evaluating projects.

SUGGESTED SOLUTION

    i.   Cost of equity

$$Ke = \frac{d}{MVex\text{-}div} \times 100\%$$

$$= \frac{0.10}{0.75} \times 100\%$$

$$= 0.1333 \times 100\%$$

$$= 13.33\%$$

    ii.   Cost of loan stock.

$$Kd = \frac{i}{MVex\text{-}div} \times 100\%$$

$$= \frac{12}{80} \times 100\%$$

$$= 0.15 \times 100\%$$

$$= 15\%$$

iii.   Weighted Average Cost of Capital (WACC)

Sources of capital	a C.O.C	b MKV(£)	a x b Total (£)
Equity	13.33%	150,000	19,995
Loan Stock	15%	80,000	12,000
		230,000	31,995

$$\text{WACC} = \frac{£31,995}{£230,000} \times 100\%$$

$$= 13.91\%$$

The weighted average cost of capital is 13.91%.

Workings:

Computation of market value

Market value of Equity:

200,000 ×£0.75 = £150,000

Market value of Loan Stock:

$$\frac{100,000}{100} \times £80 = £80,000$$

Note:

C.O.C represents "Cost of capital".

MKV represents "market value".

WACC represents weighted average cost of capital.

b) The relevant and ideal cost of capital to be used in evaluating project is weighted average cost of capital (WACC) because it involves all components of capital structure. The WACC from the calculation above is 13.91%.

REFERENCES:

www.accountinghour.com

ICAN (Strategic Financial Management)

www.ingramcontent.com/pod-product-compliance
Lightning Source LLC
Chambersburg PA
CBHW070926180526
45168CB00005B/2167